MONOLOGUES FOR KIDS

RUTH MAE RODDY

Dramaline® Publications

NOTE: "Monologues For Kids" may be utilized for workshop, audition, special readings, and class work purposes without royalty consideration. If however, they are presented either individually, or in total, before an audience where admission is charged, royalty payment is required. Contact publisher for applicable rates.

Dramaline Publications
36-851 Palm View Road
Rancho Mirage, CA 92270
Phone 760-770-6076 Fax: 760-770-4507
Web: dramaline.com E-mail: drama.line@verizon.net

ISBN-10: 0-940669-02-1
ISBN-13: 978-0-940669-02-4

Cover graphics by Kristin Deasy, age 7.

This book is printed on paper that meets the requirements of the American Standard of Permanance of paper printed for library material.

CONTENTS

GIRLS

WORKSHEET

LISA

Lisa loves visiting her grandparents.

My grandmother and grandfather live in this great big huge condo. It has a big iron gate in front and you have to buzz a buzzer to get in. They have an elevator and I always push all the buttons which really bugs my dad because we have to stop on every floor. And they have all kinds of neat stuff at their place for me to play with when I come over. Stuff like crayons and paints and books and a whole bunch of neat video games. The last time I was over I got to help my grandmother make chocolate chip cookies. She let me help her mix stuff with her electric mixer. It was really fun and she didn't yell at me once. Not like at home. That's what's so neat about going over to their place—they let you help out and do things and fool around and stuff, and if you make a mess or goof up they don't go crazy. My grandfather even lets me help him wash his car. It's fun. Except my feet usually get all wet and after awhile I get pretty tired. Washing cars is okay if you don't have to do the whole thing.

My grandma and grandpa always spend a lot of time with me and we talk and mess around and do all kinds of stuff together. That's the best thing about going to your grandparent's house—they make you feel special.

WORKSHEET

_____

_____

_____

_____

_____

_____

_____

_____

_____

_____

_____

_____

CINDY

Cindy is ambivalent regarding her feelings for her brother.

Sometimes Roger is nice. But most of the time he's a real nerd and treats me creepy and when I tell Mom he tells her he didn't do anything and that I'm a crybaby. I think older brothers like to be mean to their sisters. Like Darla Woodruff's brother—he's always treating her mean and stuff. Last week he locked her in their garage. Then he and his ratty friends made all kinds of scary noises and told her that there were monsters in there that were going to eat her up.

Sometimes, though, Roger helps me and takes care of me and watches out for me. Like when we walk home from school he always takes my hand when we cross the street. And, like, one time when this kid made fun of me he beat him up. But then, after being real nice, he always goes and messes it up by being mean or scaring me or yelling at me, or something. Yesterday he hid my dolls and told me someone had broken into our house and taken them. I told Mom and she yelled at him and made him give them back. Creep.

I asked Mom why Roger treats me mean a lot and she said it's because he loves me. (*Thoughtful pause.*) Sometimes I wish Roger didn't love me so much.

WORKSHEET

DORIS

Doris relates her sleeping out adventure.

Last week Alice and I made a tent in the backyard out of old blankets. We put them over the clothesline and fastened them to the ground with wooden sticks. It was real big tent and on the inside it was nice and cosy. We put a bunch more blankets inside for a floor and then put a bunch of our stuff in there: our dolls and books and games and stuff. We played in the tent all day and even ate our lunch and dinner in it and everything.

We asked our moms if we could sleep out in the tent all night and they said yes and we got some more blankets and our pillows and made beds. We sat in the tent and talked and listened to the radio till real late and Daddy brought us out some popcorn and Cokes. When it got too late Mom told us to turn out our flashlights and go to sleep.

We tried to sleep but we couldn't. We kept hearing these funny noises. Alice said that maybe it was monsters and big animals and we got scared. Outside the tent everything was real dark and strange and spooky looking and Alice started to cry and wanted her mom and wanted to go home. We tried to stay in the tent but it was too weird so we went inside and slept in my room. With the lights on.

WORKSHEET

BETTY

Frustrated and threatened by her parent's separation, Betty's feelings surface during this outpouring to her father.

You didn't have to go and leave, Dad! You didn't have to! You could have stayed and everything would be just like always and all of us would be happy.

Like, everything's real creepy now. Ever since you went away and moved into that dumb old apartment. Gee whiz! And now the only time I get to see you is on Saturdays and Sundays and holidays and stuff.

And now Mom has this crumby job and I've got this creepy old woman taking care of me and bossing me around all the time. I hate her! And Mom has her dumb old boyfriend hanging around the house all the time. He sits in your chair and eats with us and acts like he owns the place, or something. I don't like him. I hate him! I don't like anyone else in our house but you.

When you and I do stuff together it's not like it was before; not like it was when you were home and all of us used to do stuff together. Then it was fun. Now—now it's awful. Nothing's any fun anymore.

Come on back home. Please! I know you and Mom still like each other, I just know you do. You just have to—because you're my parents.

WORKSHEET

_____

_____

_____

_____

_____

_____

_____

_____

_____

_____

_____

_____

CAROL

Carol dreads the anxiety of parental retribution.

Whenever I do something wrong, Mom makes me go to my room and wait for my Dad. I just wish she'd just go ahead and punish me and get it over with. That way it would be easy; that way you don't have to sit in your room all day and worry about what your dad's going to do when he comes home.

Daddy never says anything to me right away. He always makes it worse by waiting till after dinner to yell and stuff. I think he likes being mean better on a full stomach. He always takes me to my room and closes the door so no one else can hear him being a creep. Than he always asks me why I did what I did. Gee whiz . . . if I knew that, and knew it was going to get me in trouble, I wouldn't have done it in the first place, would I? Anyway, he always listens to me real polite and then he scolds me and makes me feel awful. Sometimes he punishes me by making me do a whole bunch of work around the house. Or he'll ground me or make me go to bed real early.

I hate going to bed early because then I can't watch TV or mess with the computer. And it always seems like every time I have to go to bed early is when all my favorite shows are on.

I'm gonna have to start remembering not to goof up on the days when good stuff's on TV.

WORKSHEET

MOLLY

Molly bemoans her piano lessons.

Like, I have to take these stupid piano lessons every Wednesday after school. From old Mrs. Campbell. She's like this big tall lady who lives over on Euclid Avenue. She has a great big grand piano in her living room where she teaches a whole bunch of kids. Her house is always freezing cold in the winter. (*She shivers.*) Mrs. Campbell sits next to me on the piano bench and yells at me when I make a mistake. I hate piano lessons and I tell my mom I do but she doesn't listen. Nobody listens to kids.

I'm in the beginners' book. It's supposed to be real easy, but it isn't. It's real hard. The hardest part for me is trying to keep the right time. I can't. Even though Mrs. Campbell counts out loud. (*She impersonates Mrs. Campbell counting aloud.*) "One-two-three-four, one-two-three-four." So far, after almost a year, all I can play are these dumb little pieces. Mostly only with my right hand. My left hand doesn't work right. (*She makes awkward, piano playing movements with her left hand.*)

I have to practice every day, too. While other kids are out playing, I have to stay in and and do my piano lesson. I keep telling Mom how much I hate it but she says I have talent. Know what? Having talent isn't any fun.

13

WORKSHEET

KRISTIN

Kristin love pets. Here she describes her menagerie.

My dog's name is Fluffy. I call him fluffy because he fell in the dryer when he was a puppy and his fur got all weird and fuzzy. Kittywitty, my cat, I found in a dumpster on a vacant lot. She's real skinny and white and has a long nose and my dad says she looks like a ferret. But she's real neat and does these neat tricks like rolling over and sitting up—like a dog does. But she's a cat. This is what makes her neat.

I have a bird, too. Named, Pepper. We keep him in a cage in our den. One time, when I had him out playing with him, he got loose and made a mess all over the house that smelled bad for a long time.

My pet turtle's name is Floyd. I named him after my favorite uncle who kinda looks like a turtle himself. We got him at the five and dime store. He stays in a plastic bowl we keep in the kitchen window. He loves the sun and stretches his neck and legs way out just like he's sunbathing. He sleeps a lot and sometimes it's hard to tell if he's dead or alive.

I had another cat but he got run over by a United Parcel truck. I buried him under a rose bush. That's the only trouble with pets. You get to like them a lot and when something happens to them it makes you real sad.

15

WORKSHEET

JANICE

Jancie longs for earlier times; times when her father wasn't encumbered with business and preoccupied with success.

Lately, when my dad comes home at night, he's always real tired and funny acting. And sometimes he's real grouchy. When he's like that—really grumpy—Mom calls him a grouch and makes this real ugly grouchy face at him. Like this . . . (*She imitates her mother's "grouchy" face.*)

Lots of nights Daddy's real quiet and doesn't say much and acts like he's someplace else. And during dinner, when you talk to him, he doesn't seem to hear. Then there are nights when he spends the whole evening on the phone talking business to people. Mom says it's because he's real busy working hard to make money so we can have nice things and so me and my brothers and sisters can go to college. She says that when Daddy was a little kid, his family was real poor and he never had much; like toys and new clothes or a nice house, or anything.

Sometimes, though, I think he works way too hard. And he doesn't play around anymore like he used to. He used to come home early and mess around with us kids and watch TV with us, and stuff, and was friendly and nice.

It seems like when people get successful they aren't any fun anymore.

17

WORKSHEET

ERIN

Erin tells her best friend about her upcoming special day—her birthday.

On my birthday, I get to do anything I want. For the whole day. Mom said I could.(*Pause for response.*) Sure, are you kidding? Of course you're invited. You an Betty Clark and Sally Green and Samantha Oliver and Susie Goldman and Maria Gonzales and Charlene White and Candy Sommers. I'm not inviting any boys. Boys make too much noise and run around and tear things up and show off and won't play the games right.

First we're gonna go ice skating and then go to a movie and then, after the movie, to McDonald's. Mom's got it all planned. Then we're coming back here and have ice cream and cake and open the presents. Mom's got this magician coming to do a whole bunch of tricks. She said he does this one trick where he puts a dove in a bag (*Demonstrates.*) and then smashes the bag and then opens it and the dove is gone. (*She cringes.*) I think I'll ask 'im not to do that trick.

Birthdays are neat because I get to do anything I want and I get presents. My dad says he doesn't like birthdays because they remind him he's getting old. I can't wait to get old. When you're sixteen you get to do all kinds of neat stuff.

WORKSHEET

MEGAN

Megan, a girl with family hardships, is enriched in many ways.

Sometimes I wish I had new toys and clothes and things but I can't because my father is sick. He can't work anymore like he used to. My mom works part-time now and takes care of us the best she can. She works at the shoe factory over on Spring Street. When she comes home she's real tired, and after supper's over, she sits in her chair and falls asleep.

Daddy got hurt real bad in a car wreck and now he can't walk. He has to stay in a wheelchair all the time. He makes these cute little toys out of scrap wood they have down at Henderson's Lumber Company.

My sister, Julie, and my brother, Harry, and I do lots of work around the house and help out so it's easier for my mom. We do stuff for dad, too. We run errands for him and get him wood and go along places with him in his wheelchair. Yesterday we all went down to the river to watch the boats and barges. It was fun. My father is a nice man.

And my mom's nice, too, even though she's busy. And she really loves my dad. They love each other. You can tell by the way they treat each other. There's a lot of love in our house which more than makes up for not having all kinds of stuff. I wouldn't trade places with anybody. I think my family's the best family in the whole world.

WORKSHEET

MINDY

Mindy reflects on child abuse.

On TV there was this thing about this little kid whose parents beat her up all the time. She was real little and skinny and didn't look like she got enough to eat. She had these great big red and blue places all over her back and arms where her mother hit her with a coat hanger wire. It was awful. I almost cried.

My mom said that lots of kids get beat up by their parents and are mistreated by them. I don't know why anyone would want to beat up on a little kid. Little kids are helpless and can't get away or fight back. Anyone who mistreats a kid is a bad person and shouldn't be allowed to have children at all. I guess there are lots of mean people in this world; people who don't care about other people, you know? about what they think or feel.

If I have kids, I'm going to treat them extra nice. Because I know how important it is to have a mom and dad who care about you and love you and make you feel special—like mine.

I wish we could take all the kids who are being hurt away from the people who are hurting them and give them nice homes and make them feel loved and not afraid. I don't think anybody should be made to feel afraid—anybody.

WORKSHEET

_____

_____

_____

_____

_____

_____

_____

_____

_____

_____

_____

_____

AMY

Amy finds abhorrent the violence on TV.

Every time I watch TV it seems like someone is getting shot, or killed, or beat up, or something. Gross! Almost every show has people getting pounded on or wasted. Yuck!

My mom wrote this letter to the television stations and complained about all the killing and stuff and they wrote her back, but she didn't like what they said. They said they thought their shows are okay.

I try to watch shows that don't have anyone getting killed or have scary nerds running around cutting people up. I watch "Sesame Street" and some of the old shows like "Leave it to Beaver," and that. My parents rent us movies, too. My favorite is *The Sound of Music.* I like the old Lassie movies a lot, too, and all the stuff with Haley Mills. Especially *Pollyanna,* where she comes to this town and makes it happy. Neat.

My brother watches all the police stuff where people are always getting zapped. He gets mad when I want to turn them off and watch my stuff on the VCR. He thinks "Pollyanna" is lame. I think that's because he's older. Older people have trouble liking things that are nice.

WORKSHEET

KAREN

Karen doesn't comprehend her mother's penchant for neatness.

It's, like, I'm never supposed to get dirty, right? I'm supposed to stay clean all the time and never get messed up. Hey! nobody can stay clean *all* the time. It doesn't make sense. But my mom expects me to never get even the littlest teeny-weeny speck of anthing on me—*ever!* Is she kidding, or what?

Last week Mary Sanders and I cut through the vacant lot and guess what? I have to go and trip over something and fall down and really gross out my new jacket. Wow! A real mess. It had these big hunks of mud on it and it was all wet and stained and everything. I felt like crying because I knew I was gonna get yelled at good good when I got home.

We went over to Mary's and tried to clean it up with some stuff her mom had but it just made it look all smeary and worse than ever.

When I got home, Mom really yelled at me bad. I tried to tell her it was an accident but she wouldn't listen. I mean . . . is it my fault I tripped? Gimme a break! Everybody has an accident now and then—everybody. Even grownups, even if they won't admit it. To hear them tell it, kids are the only ones who ever goof up. Hey! all you have to do is look around to see how bad grownups mess up the world every single day.

WORKSHEET

KATY

Katy speaks affectionately of a former neighbor.

Mrs. Murray lived over on the next street. She used to walk her little dog all the time. She walked real slow because she was crippled and it took her a long time to make it around to block. I used to see her and talk to her almost every day. We talked about all kinds of stuff and she always listened to me like what I had to say was important.

Last week I saw this ambulance in front of her place. Right away I knew something was wrong. Mom told me that she was real sick and that they had to put her in the hospital. I went over see her there and she was sitting up in bed and she looked real nice in a pretty pink nightgown. I told her we were taking care of her dog and she said she was glad and that she missed him. It was a neat visit and she still seemed interested in me even though she was sick. She asked me to come see her again.

Mom said Mrs. Murray died last night. I'm very sad and already miss her a whole lot. It just won't seem the same without her around and now the neighborhood has like this great big hole in it that she used to fill. She was a nice lady. And I'll always remember this about her . . . even though she was crippled and sick she never complained. She was always smiling.

WORKSHEET

BOYS

WORKSHEET

MIKE

Mike finds silly his mother's and her friends' "girl talk."

When my mom has her friends over, they all get in the kitchen and drink coffee and talk about stupid junk. And they all talk at the same time and I have to go to my room and close the door because their voices make this terrible sound like a bunch of gerbils. And they say kids make noise. Give me a break! At least kids don't go talking real fast and loud at the same time about nothing.

And they always talk about how everything is cute, ya konw? Like *cute* dresses and *cute* hats and *cute* shoes.

My mom said saw saw this *cute* dress and that it would be *cute* for my sister, Ann, to wear because she's going to this big wedding. She said it would look *cute* with some *cute* shoes she saw and this *cute* purse. She said Ann would be like the *cutest* girl at the wedding because she would be wearing all this *cute* stuff and would have her hair fixed *cute,*too. All of Mom's friends said that it really sounded *cute.* Sometimes I think Mom and her friends are spaced.

I asked dad about all the cute talk and he didn't say anything. He just stared off real glassy-eyed like he does when Mom talks to him about having her mother move in with us.

WORKSHEET

ERIC

Eric, an only child, is wary about the arrival of a new brother.

Guess what? My mom's gonna have a baby. (*Pause.*)
Yeah, and pretty soon, too. Haven't you noticed how
big and puffed up she is and how funny she walks?
That's because she's pregnant. Dad thinks she looks
pretty. To me she looks pretty weird.
Mom and Dad have been going to these classes
where they're learning how Mom can have the baby
without being knocked out. They practice breathing
and stuff.
And they've already named him, too—Rodney.
Wow. It that a nerd name, or what? (*Pause for listen-
ing.*) Yeah, they already know it's gong to be a boy
because they had his test done and found out. They
wanted to know so they could plan ahead. Like buying clothes and how to fix up the room.
Since Mom got pregnant, it's like I'm not even here
anymore, okay? All they've got time for now is stupid
classes and buying stuff and talking about the baby all
the time. Everything's crummy and messed up now
and it's like my home's not even my home anymore.
When they ask me if I'm happy about the baby, I tell
them Yes because I don't wanna take a chance of getting it, ya know? But hey! who needs a brother?
Especially one named Rodney. *Rodney? Are they
kidding?*

WORKSHEET

ANDY

Andy thinks his parents are nice. Well...most of the time, anyway.

My parents are nice. I like them a lot. They treat me nice and let me play and mess around and do most of the stuff I want. I'm lucky. Some kid's parents are all the time yelling at them and slapping them around. People who slap kids around are creeps. They shouldn't be allowed to have kids in the first place.

Once in a while my folks yell at me, too. But usually, it's because I goof up or don't do what they ask me to do—like, clean up my room or help out around the house. Sometimes you forget to do stuff because you're too busy playing and stuff. The other day I left my bike out in the drive, and when my dad came home he had to get out of his car and move it before he could put his car in the garage. That was the second time in a week. He said the next time he's going to run over it. Sometimes my parents get carried away, too. But most of the time they're cool.

It's real important that you mind your parents and help out at home and not goof off and be a stupe. After all, they take care of you and spend lots of money on you till you're grown up. I like my parents and I really appreciate all the things they do. My parents are great—most of the time.

WORKSHEET

RALPH

Ralph speaks to his father's girlfriend's daughter regarding the complication of their parents marrying.

What if my dad married your mom? You ever think about that? Would you want me for a brother? Or half-brother, or whatever? (*Pause.*) Um, me too, I don't know for sure, either. I mean . . . I don't know if I'd want you for a sister, you know? I mean, like, you're okay and all that but . . . but, like, if it would come to living in the same house and everything . . . besides, you wouldn't be my *real* sister.

I like your mom a lot but I don't know if I'd like her yelling at me and bossing me around, you know? Just like it'd be for you if my dad bossed you. I mean . . . . they're not our real parents. And anyway, I don't know if I like the idea of my dad getting married again, anyway. Maybe my mother wouldn't like me anymore if I was living here with your mom. Like, how do you think *your* dad would feel? (*Pause for response.*) Yeah . . . that's what I think, too.

I think people are nuts for getting married again, anyhow. I mean, if you goof up the first time, why would you wanna take the chance of goofing up again?

WORKSHEET

_____

_____

_____

_____

_____

_____

_____

_____

_____

_____

_____

_____

ERNIE

Ernie, an unwilling rider, tells of motor trips with Mom and Dad.

I hate going places with my mom and dad in the car. I try to get out of going, but they make me go along anyway. On these real long trips. I have to sit in the back seat and listen to them talk about a bunch of lame junk. And Mom and Dad argue all the time because Dad screams at other drivers and calls them bad names and this makes her mad. I fact, they seem to argue all the time. About stupid stuff. Grownups don't make much sense a lot, you know?

Sometimes we take my aunt Helen along with us. The pits. She always has to kiss me and tell me how much I've grown even though it's only been a couple of weeks since she's seen me. Weird. And she's real fat and she smells awful because she wears tons of barfy perfume. And she messes with my hair, too—tries to make it lay down flat. I *hate* having spit rubbed into my head. Wow!

Last Sunday we take this drive and get lost and Mom and Dad really got into it because we had to get back home before our dinner burned up. Dad got real crazy and started banging the steering wheel and swearing because we were stuck in all this traffic. When we finally got home dinner was ruined. Which was okay with me because we got to go to McDonald's instead of eating roast lamb.

WORKSHEET

BOBBY

Bobby has a pretty good understanding of a person's need to lie.

Last week my dad's uncle, Dave, came to visit. He has a neat car and wears these far-out suits and smokes these huge cigars that are longer than your arm. He slept in my room in the spare bed and snored like a bear and it really bugged me.

He told me a bunch of stories about when he was in the army and how he fought Germans. He said he was like this big hero who saved a zillion lives. He showed me this scar where he got wounded—*gross!* He told me about when he went fishing in Mexico, too, and how he'd caught the biggest shark ever caught by anyone. He showed me a picture of him with the shark. It had jaws as big as this room.

After he left, Dad said that his Uncle Dave really wasn't ever in the war and that he wasn't a hero and that the scar was from this time he wiped out on his motorcycle. And he said he'd never ever caught a shark and that the picture he carries around he had taken with this big stuffed fish they have for guys who don't catch fish but like to say they do. Dad said Dave is a cool guy but he likes to make up stories a lot. (*Pause.*) He's like this kid at school, Bobby Wheeler, who likes to make up big deal stuff all the time. I think he does it so people will like him. Poor guy. (*Pause.*) I guess grownups need people to like them, too.

WORKSHEET

CHARLES

Charles voices his protestations regarding performing at a school function.

Aw, gee whiz, Mom—I can't! I can't get up and sing in front of a whole bunch of people. (*Pause.*) I don't know why, I just can't, that's all. I makes me feel funny. And with you and Dad watching it'll be even worse. (*Pause.*) I don't care . . . I'm not gonna do it! I hate it more than anything. When I get up in front of people I always feel great big and puffy and like everybody's staring at just *me!*And besides, most of my class is girls. Who want's to get up with a bunch of stupid girls, anyhow? And I have to stand next to that big rat, Charlotte Adams. She's great big and horsey with all this hair on her arms and a voice like a frog's. (*Mimics her singing in a very deep, comical voice.*)

And we have to dress up like nerds, too. We have to wear these paper bags on our heads painted to make us look like these robots from outer space. And then we have to sing these awful songs: "We've Only Just Begun," and "Up Up And Away." Stuff nobody ever heard of.

Hey!I don't care if Grandma's coming, or not. I'm still not gonna do it. I'll sit out front with you guys and act like *I'm* having fun, too.

WORKSHEET

BRIAN

Brian enumerates the advantages of illness.

Every once in a while I get a bad cold and they make me stay home and take medicine and stuff. I hate taking cough medicine because it get's stuck in my throat like this big glob of thick grease. (*He affects coughing.*) But taking medicine's better than having to go to the doctor and getting this dry stick rammed down your throat and needles jamed in your arm.

When I'm sick, everybody treats me nice. Even my sister, Joyce. Nobody yells at you when you're sick. You can get away with all kinds of stuff if you've got a fever. Your parents wait to you're well before they start being mean to you again. My grandparents aways call me up when I'm sick, too. And sometimes they come over and bring presents. Last winter, when I had the flu, they brought over some neat vieos and CDs.

And my mom always makes me my favorite stuff to eat then, too. Like chocolate pudding with whipped cream, cookies, and all the neat food that doesn't taste like wood—like the stuff they usually want you to eat when you're feeling good.

But the best thing about being sick is that you don't have to go to school. You can just lie around in your pajamas all day and watch TV. And surf the Web. Ya know . . . I think sometimes being sick is almost better than being well.

WORKSHEET

_____

_____

_____

_____

_____

_____

_____

_____

_____

_____

_____

_____

TEDDY

Teddy is confronted with the mystique of the fairer sex.

Like, there's this new girl in school, okay? Her name is Sally Cartwright. She just moved here from Chcago. She's real pretty and wears cool clothes. And she doesn't talk to the rest of the kids much—just me. She asks me all kinds of stuff about school and about the other kids and about where I live, about the kind of movies and music I like, and junk—everything. Yesterday she asked me to give her a shove in a swing. I didn't want to, but I didn't want her to think I didn't like her, either, ya know? I like her okay, I guess, I just wish she wouldn't bug me so much, that's all, because it makes me feel funny in front of the other kids. I told Mom and she said I should always be friendly no matter what anybody else thinks. I dunno. It's real hard not to care about what other people think.

I just wish Sally would stop following me around all the time and smiling at me with this smile that makes me feel weird in this way I can't explain. Besides, girls kinda give me the creeps a lot anyway—especially the pretty ones. I wish Sally was ugly with big horsey yellow teeth with braces like Erma Long. That way maybe she wouldn't make me feel so weird.

WORKSHEET

DANNY

Danny expresses the trauma of being a newcomer.

We came here from Springfield last summer. My dad got a better job so we had to move. All my friends are back in Springfield: Frank McKinnon, Richard Lawrence, Ace McCann . . . everybody. But here, here I don't know anybody. I don't have anyone to mess around with. I just stay home and watch TV and listen to my sister talk stupid on the phone.

I don't know any of the guys in school, either. And nobody's friendly. My dad says people are like that when you're new, even to him, and that it takes a while for them to find out about you and get to know you. But it's, a lot harder for kids to make friends than grownups because kids are honest and say the stuff that's on their mind. And sometimes what's on their mind hurts your feelings. Like when a bunch of 'em said my clothes looked like I got them from the homeless. Creeps!

Back home I had lots of friends in school and all kinds of kids to walk home with and mess around with later. Here I have to walk home alone and then hang around the house a listen to my sister talk like a weasel.

Hey! It's not any fun being lonely.

WORKSHEET

MICHAEL

He relates a recent medical incident.

(*Rolling up his shirt sleeve.*) Here . . . let me show you where I got my shot. See it? It's the red place that's kinda all bumpy and red and weird. See it?

Mom and Dad didn't say where we were going. They just said we had to go someplace and that it was important. I knew it had to be something super-bad, because when they keep stuff secret, it usually is.

As soon as I saw the building I knew they were taking me to the doctor, because it was the same building we took my sister to to get stitches the time she busted her head open on the coffee table. Right away I started to get sick and my legs felt funny. When I started to yell they told me I had to get this shot that all kids have to get. A shot! Like, wow!

The doctor was a real monster and you could tell right away he liked to hurt people. Besides, why else would he want to be a doctor? He told me to roll up my sleeve but I wouldn't so my dad rolled it up and then my mom held me so I couldn't run or kick or anything. Then the doctor jabbed me in arm with this big, huge, long needle and I yelled but he didn't care because he loves to hear kids scream. (*Pause.*) Afterwards they bought me a hot fudge so maybe I wouldn't hate them anymore.

WORKSHEET

CLAVIN

Calvin contemplates his adult life, touches on the loss of dreams.

When I grow up I wanna be an astronaut. Because I think outerspace is cool. Like in the Star Trek movies where they get to explore the universe and have these neat adventures. Except real astronauts don't get to do the things the Enterprise guys do because their stuff is real and not made up by some clown.

My dad is an accountant. He works in his den with his calculator a lot, and lots of times, when I go to bed, he's still there working. I don't think he has much fun. Besides, being an accountant isn't very cool. (*Pause.*) I used to think being a cowboy would be cool. But there aren't any cowboys anymore. Not like in the old days. Today cowboys chase steers with SUVs. (*Pause.*) I think being a pro football payer would be cool. Except you have to be big and strong and I don't know if I'm going to be big or not. I may grown up to be little.

My dad said he always wanted to be a forest ranger—now he's an accountant. My Uncle Ralph wanted to be a sailor—he sells real estate. My best friend's dad wanted to be a pilot—he's an insurance adjuster. I don't think being an insurance adjuster is very cool at all. Know what? Seems like all the grownups I know never got to be what they wanted.

WORKSHEET

ADAM

Adam tells of the rigors of participating in the class photo.

Last week they took our class picture. I hated it. I had to, like, wear my good clothes and I couldn't play all day because if I got them dirty or tore them my mom would really go crazy and yell—or worse, even. Oh yeah, I had to wear this dumb tie, too. (*Feigns gagging.*) I hate ties. My dad wears one every day. No wonder he's grouchy.

Mrs. Smith had us all line up and we had to march down to the gym where the guy who took the picture had his camera stuff set up. He had us line up in rows —littlest kids in front, tallest kids in the back. Janet Clark had to stand in the back because she's bigger than anyone—Mrs. Smith, even. Janet Clark is a big goon.

Every single time the guy tried to take our picture somebody would move or goof-up, or something, and we'd have to start all over. Corky Johnson kept making this real funny face like a beaver and kept cracking everyone up. Ms. Smith made him leave. Boy, was he ever lucky. Only thing is—what's he gonna tell his mom and dad when they see the class picture and he's not in it. Oh, boy.

We got our picture back today. My mom hates it because part of my head is missing because of Janet Clark's arm. Big deal.

WORKSHEET

BILLY

He relates his vacation adventure.

This last summer we drove out to California. My mom and dad and my sister, Judy, and I. It was a long trip and Judy and I slept in the back seat on pillows a lot. Judy kept getting carsick all the time. Like, yuck! (*Pause.*) The Rocky Mountains were really high and some of the peaks still had snow on them. On the Fourth of July we stopped and made snowballs. Once we got over the mountains there was the desert, and it was totally hot and dry and you could see nothing for miles. I was so hot the car overheated and we had to stop way out in the middle of nowhere. My mom got scared because she said we didn't have any water and that we'd all die of thirst and turn to skeletons. Sometimes she's off the wall, ya know? (*Pause.*) Anyway, it got really hot, and there wasn't anyone around because we'd gone off the interstate to see this Indian trading post where there weren't any Indians—just a bunch of cheap junk. And then Judy started to freak because she said she thought she saw some Indians in the rocks and, like, they were gonna get us and torture us and scalp us and everything. She gets this from from my Mom.

After a while, this real dried up old guy in a beat up truck comes along and tows us to a service station where we get water and Cokes. (*Pause.*) The next time we go to California—I wanna fly.

ORDER DIRECT

A WOMAN SPEAKS: WOMEN FAMOUS, INFAMOUS and UNKNOWN, ed. Cosentino. $12.95.
BETH HENLEY: MONOLOGUES for WOMEN, Henley. *Crimes of the Heart*, others. $9.95.
CITY WOMEN, Smith. $9.95.
CLASSIC MOUTH, ed. Cosentino. Speeches for kids from famous literature. $8.95.
COLD READING and HOW to BE GOOD at IT, Hoffman. $12.95.
DIALECT MONOLOGUES, Karshner/Stern. Book and cassette tape. $19.95.
DIALECT MONOLOGUES, VOL. II, Karshner/Stern. Book and cassette tape. $19.95.
DIALECT MONOLOGUES—CD VERSION, Karshner/Stern. $22.95.
FITTING IN. Monologues for kids, Mauro. $8.95.
FOR WOMEN: MONOLOGUES THEY HAVEN'T HEARD, Pomerance. $9.95.
FOR WOMEN: MORE MONOS THEY HAVEN'T HEARD, Pomerance. $9.95.
FOR WOMEN: POCKET MONOLOGUES from SHAKESPEARE, Dotterer. $9.95.
HIGH-SCHOOL MONOLOGUES THEY HAVEN'T HEARD, Karshner. $9.95.
KIDS' STUFF, Roddy. 30 great audition pieces for children. $9.95.
KNAVES, KNIGHTS, and KINGS, ed. Dotterer. Shakespeare's speeches for men. $8.95.
MINUTE MONOLOGUES for KIDS, Roddy. $9.95.
MODERN MONOLOGUES for MODERN KIDS, Mauro. $9.95.
MODERN SCENES for WOMEN, Pomerance. Scenes for today's actresses. $7.95.
MONOLOGUES for KIDS, Roddy. 28 wonderful speeches for boys and girls. $9.95.
MONOLOGUES for TEENAGE GIRLS, Pomerance. $9.95.
MONOLOGUES for TEENAGERS, Karshner. Contemporary teen speeches. $9.95.
MONOLOGUES for WOMEN, Pomerance. $9.95.
MONOLOGUES from CHEKHOV, trans. Cartwright. $8.95.
MONOLOGUES from GEORGE BERNARD SHAW, ed. Michaels. $7.95.
MONOLOGUES from MOLIERE, trans. Dotterer. $9.95.
MONOLOGUES from OSCAR WILDE, ed. Michaels. $7.95.
MONOLOGUES from the CLASSICS, ed. Karshner. $8.95.
MONOLOGUES THEY HAVEN'T HEARD, Karshner. Speeches for men and women. $9.95.
MORE MONOLOGUES HAVEN'T HEARD, Karshner. More living-language speeches. $9.95.
MORE MONOLOGUES for KIDS, Roddy. More great speeches for boys and girls. $9.95.
MORE MONOLOGUES for TEENAGERS, Karshner. $9.95.
NEIL SIMON MONOLOGUES, ed. Karshner. $14.95.
NEIL SIMON SCENES, ed. Karshner. $14.95.
POCKET MONOLOGUES for MEN, Karshner. $9.95.
POCKET MONOLOGUES for WOMEN, Pomerance. 30 modern speeches. $9.95.
POCKET MONOLOGUES: WORKING-CLASS CHARACTERS for WOMEN, Pomerance. $8.95.
RED LICORICE, Tippit. 31 great scene-monologues for preteens. $9.95.
SCENES for KIDS, Roddy. 30 scenes for girls and boys. $9.95.
SCENES for TEENAGERS, Karshner. Scenes for today's teen boys and girls. $9.95.
SHAKESPEARE'S LADIES, ed. Dotterer. $9.95.
SHAKESPEARE'S MONOLOGUES for WOMEN, ed. Dotterer. $9.95.
SHAKESPEARE'S MONOLOGUES THEY HAVEN'T HEARD, ed. Dotterer. $9.95.
TEENAGE MOUTH, Karshner. Modern monologues for young men and women. $9.95.
VOICES. Speeches from the writings of famous women, ed. Cosentino. $12.95.
WHEN KIDS ACHIEVE, Mauro. Positive monologues for preteen boys and girls. $8.95.
WOMAN, Pomerance. Monologues for actresses. $8.95.
YOU SAID a MOUTHFUL, Karshner. Tongue twisters galore. $8.95.

For details visit our on-line catalog at: dramaline.com

Send your check or money order (no cash or COD) plus handling charges of $4.00 for the first book and $1.50 for each additional book. California residents add 8.25 % tax. Send your order to: Dramaline Publications, 36-851 Palm View Road, Ranch Mirage, California 92270-2417.